Twisted: Mindful Pretzel Consumption

Jill Marie Thomas

(Great-great-granddaughter of Julius Sturgis, founder of America's first commercial pretzel bakery)

Sharon,
Happy snacking!
Jill Marie Thomas

ISBN: 9781077654914

First printing edition 2019.

ww.jillmariethomas.com

Pretzel illustrations by:
Keturah Martin, kittyturah@gmail.com

Interior and cover design by:
Sue A. Fairchild, sueafairchild74@gmail.com

To my dad, Tom Sturgis:
You taught me everything I know
about pretzels …
and much about life too.
I'm grateful, and I love you.

Contents

Acknowledgments

Words on a page seem so inadequate, but please know they come from my heart deep with gratitude to…

My editor and friend, Marsha Hubler. With diligence and patience, you correct and teach me to be a better writer. I love the friendship we are developing too.

Sue Fairchild, for your creative assistance and expertise in formatting my writing into book form. Your own writing and editing background proved invaluable, but your commitment to be my prayer buddy has made all the difference.

My great-great grandfather, Julius Sturgis, who established America's first commercial pretzel bakery and left behind an incredible legacy and career path for succeeding generations of our family.

My grandfather, Marriott "Tom" Sturgis, for establishing Tom Sturgis Pretzels. Despite having only an eighth-grade education, he taught us the value of working hard through many difficulties, and he entertained us and endowed us with his quirky wisdom.

My father, Tom Sturgis. Best father ever. Period. Thank you for carrying on the art of making the best pretzels anywhere and for taking care of our family so well over all the years and to this day.

My mother, Barbara Sturgis, for continually believing in me and suggesting over many years that I should write about our family's heritage with pretzels. Thanks, Mom. Here it is, finally.

My younger brothers, Bruce and Chris. I loved growing up with you and being the oldest and wisest. We ate lots of pretzels in our home and could not have had a better childhood together.

My four children, Rachel, Lindsay, Sarah, and Caleb, who appreciate being sixth generation Sturgis family members and always encourage me to keep writing.

My husband, Bob, who is my biggest cheerleader and who thinks I'm way more capable of doing anything than I ever think I am.

My Wonderful Lord—God the Father, Jesus the Son, and the Holy Spirit. I love how Your three-in-one nature is so well symbolized by the three holes in every pretzel. You give my life every bit of meaning, and without You I would be nothing. I can only hope that whatever I write pleases You, now and always.

Preface

One Saturday about 55 years ago, my parents loaded up the family station wagon with extra jackets and snacks and took my two younger brothers and me on a little road trip. I was just a young gal of about six or seven.

We headed southeast from our home in Reading to the little town of Lititz, Pennsylvania, about thirty minutes away. There we visited America's first commercial pretzel bakery, the Julius Sturgis Pretzel Bakery.

While there, we looked around at the old rooms and ancient pretzel ovens. Then my great uncle Lewis Sturgis (in his late 80s but still quite smiley and spry) greeted us and guided the family over to a long, ridged, narrow table. With a twinkle in his eye, he handed me a small lump of pretzel dough. With his old rheumatic hands, he patiently showed me how to roll my little piece of dough back and forth on the table until I had a long skinny strip.

Next, he put his hands over mine and worked the magic. Together we twisted the strip into a pretzel, the first of thousands I've made in my lifetime since then.

I was amazed at what I had created!

He then presented me with a very official-looking document stating that I had learned that day to twist a pretzel. On it, he wrote the date and signed his name.

What I didn't appreciate that day and not until many years later was that I had been introduced to my very special heritage.

I was born into the lineage of the very first commercial pretzel baker, Julius Sturgis, Lewis's father. As the great-great granddaughter of Julius Sturgis, a very big part of my life would involve pretzels.

To this day, I have a lot to say about pretzels. It's time to tell the story.

Introduction

My first recollections of pretzels go all the way back to my toddlerhood. Most of the time, Dad brought home a bag or two of the pretzels he had made that day at his pretzel bakery. At my tender age of two and a half, I had no idea how much the rest of my life would revolve around pretzels. I was a content and well-loved child, and pretzels always seemed to be part of our family's everyday life.

At the time, our family lived in a simple apartment on the upper floor of a modest house in the small Pennsylvania town of Mohnton. I recall we entered the apartment by climbing a flight of steps in the rear of the building. In the backyard grew a lovely strawberry garden where I played and ate my fill of sweet, red "drawbies" while my dad "played" with his garden tools nearby.

Our evening routine ticked by like clockwork; Mom, Dad, and I ate dinner together, then Dad bathed me while Mom cleaned up dinner. Each evening at 7:00 sharp, Dad and I snuggled in our spots on the sofa, ready for the start of our favorite TV show "Clutch Cargo." With only a five-minute-long episode each evening, it was imperative to be bathed, in jammies, and ready for the start of the show.

Clutch Cargo, along with his young ward, Spinner, and their pet dachshund, Paddlefoot, traveled around the world taking on dangerous assignments. Their adventures held me spellbound! Although the series only lasted for 52 episodes over two seasons, I remember them fondly. And…I recall sharing special pretzel snacks with my dad as we watched.

When I was nearly three, my parents brought my baby brother Bruce home from the hospital. We continued with our nightly schedule, although baby Bruce seemed to have no appreciation whatsoever for the wonders of Clutch Cargo.

When I was almost five, we moved to a new home. Because we now lived closer to the pretzel bakery, Tom Sturgis Pretzels, Dad began taking my brother and me with him to work every now and then.

Bruce and I would take rides on the pretzel conveyor belts from the first-floor store area up to the third-floor baking and packing area and back down again. We giggled as our tiny behinds bumped up and down over the conveyor rollers moving us along. As we passed the second floor, we saw a pair of ladies scrubbing and stacking empty pretzel cans, readying them to be filled with fresh pretzels.

We knew our way around the factory. Staying away from the hot pretzel ovens, we'd make our way to the "fun" twisting machines, watching their pincher "fingers" pick up the strips of dough, miraculously twist them into pretzel shapes, and then drop them onto the conveyor belt. The restrictions of OSHA (Occupational Safety and Health Administration) had not yet come into effect.

Following the path of the pretzels on the belt, we'd watch until they entered the intense inferno in the oven. After five to ten minutes (depending on the thickness of the pretzel type) they'd come out the other side, and we quickly grabbed one and held it away from our bodies in the bottom of our shirts so we wouldn't burn our fingers. Once cooled, the pretzels were like fresh soft pretzels. They hadn't yet traveled into the dryer to harden.

At the end of the belt, women packed mounds of pretzels at numerous packing stations. Cans, boxes, and bags were filled by hand using large scooping tools. I thought how wondrous that all those women wore spotless white dresses and hats and always smiled at us when we showed up. And—they could eat as many pretzels as they wanted!

In the back of the factory at the shipping office and docks, Bruce and I became familiar with the supervisor and the truckers, who often offered us lollipops and other goodies. A quick hop up onto the conveyor belt and a press of the green GO button and off we'd go again heading through the plant.

During my elementary school years, Dad often got an urgent call to go to the bakery on a Saturday to fix something. Sometimes he'd take me, and Ann, the lady who tended the onsite retail store, would put me to work. I packed two pretzels into tiny plastic sleeves, small plastic baggies with one open end. Then we'd fold closed the open end and carefully arrange these sleeves into parcel post cartons to be shipped all over the United States. Finally, I'd cut the packaging tapes to exactly the right length, wet them, and seal the box edges. I felt special to have such important work.

Occasionally, my dad or grandfather took me into the office they shared. Somehow, I knew it was a place where important business happened. It even had a special secret trap door in the floor. I think they kept money and important documents in there. Occasionally, I lined up my grandfather's extensive set of pens in perfect order while he sipped his broth and ate his half sandwich out of his briefcase. Gazing around the fascinating office, I never tired of looking at the large sailfish he'd mounted on the wall.

Dad exposed us to as many aspects of the business as he could. During our high school and college years, Bruce and I, along with our younger brother Chris, worked for real paychecks doing all sorts of tasks. Mowing lawns, scrubbing the oven walls, mixing dough, baking pretzels, packing pretzels, and working retail sales, mail order sales, cost estimating, package designing, and cost analysis. We did it all!

I cannot imagine a life without pretzels. On any day, we had a variety of pretzels at home in our kitchen pantry. Our friends loved coming home after school to have after-school snacks at our house, and Mom always welcomed them.

I'm proud of the heritage my family has in the pretzel-baking world, and I feel privileged to be able to write this little book of information about pretzels for you. It's my desire that you will love pretzels as much as I do.

HISTORY

The Origin of Pretzels

Consider the pretzel—simple, scrumptious, and nutritious. People all around the world love pretzels. Have you ever wondered who created the first pretzel?

Pretzel making is quite ancient, dating back more than 1400 years. The pretzel story began about 610 A.D. in a monastery somewhere in northern Italy or southern France.

Historians believe that a monk toyed with some leftover scraps of bread dough. He twisted the ends, formed a shape resembling a child in prayer, and popped it into the oven. At that time, parents taught their children to pray with their arms crossed over their heart and their hands on their shoulders.

The monks called this delicious creation "pretiola," which means little reward, and gave these treats to the children who recited their verses and prayers well. Some say they were originally called "bracellae," the Latin term for "little arms," from which Germans later derived the word "bretzel."

Whatever they may have been called, the popularity of these twisty treats spread across all of Europe during the Middle Ages. People believed pretzels were a symbol of good luck, prosperity, and spiritual fulfillment, and often distributed them to the poor, thus providing them with both spiritual and literal sustenance.

Pretzel making took a dramatic turn in the spotlight in 1510, when Ottoman Turks attempted to invade Vienna, Austria by digging tunnels underneath the city's walls. Monks baking pretzels in the basement of a monastery heard the enemy coming, alerted the rest of the city, and then helped defeat the Turkish attack. To reward their bravery, the Austrian emperor gave the pretzel bakers their own coat of arms. Today we see pretzels on many bakery signs in Europe.

By the seventeenth century, Germany had many pretzel bakers, and the pretzel-twisting skill crossed the Atlantic with the first German and Austrian settlers, who settled in Pennsylvania around 1710 and were nicknamed the "Pennsylvania Dutch."

The first pretzels in America had a soft inside with a firm outer crust, much like our soft pretzels today. Bread bakeries made them to expand their bakery offerings and to be available as special treats.

Later, Julius Sturgis developed the first hard, crisp pretzel, and in 1861 he opened the first commercial pretzel bakery in America.

Early Pretzel Traditions

Historians have recorded when monks rewarded children with pretzels, those proud children went home from church and carefully hung their pretzels on their Christmas trees. Decorating their Christmas trees with pretzels became a special family tradition that continues in many homes today.

Over time the pretzel became a symbol of excellence. Church leaders used pretzels to reward worthy accomplishments and flourishing youth programs.

In the following centuries, the pretzel made its way into history books and European culture. The pretzel's form became a symbol of good luck, long life, and prosperity.

In medieval times the German Emperor Ludwig of Bavaria set aside special allowance for the people to have fairs at Eastertime and in the autumn. At fair time, thieves preyed on the food and merchandise wagons coming to the city.

To protect the valuable freight from robbers, a troop of citizens rode out to meet the caravans. They welcomed the incoming merchants on all the main roads leading to Frankfurt. Those guard troops brought with them large pewter pitchers of wine to refresh the weary travelers as well as a load of pretzels hanging on their spears. Those pretzels were called Geleit pretzels (Escort pretzels) and symbolized the friendly welcome and protection offered by the greeters.

In 1440, a page in Catharine of Cleves' prayer book depicted St. Bartholomew surrounded by pretzels, which were thought to bring good luck, prosperity, and spiritual wholeness.

A decade later, Germans ate pretzels and hard-boiled eggs for dinner on Good Friday, the day of fasting. The large, puffy pretzels symbolized eternal life, and the two hard-boiled eggs nestled in each of the large round curves of the pretzel represented Easter's rebirth.

The pretzel may have given birth to Easter egg hunts. German children looked for pretzels hidden in the straw lofts and barns on their family's farms. Because pretzels and eggs were used together at Easter, it was only a matter of time before the pretzel hunts transitioned into the egg hunts we enjoy to this day.

In another tradition, folks in the German city of Sigmaringen practiced the tradition of Brautelin, "ducking" newlywed husbands on Shrove Tuesday, the day before Ash Wednesday in 1480. Those men, along with husbands celebrating silver and golden wedding anniversaries, paraded through streets and threw pretzels, oranges, and candy to the crowd. Today, the men are spared the ducking, but the parades continue with fife-and-drum music and lots of good-natured teasing.

A wood carving dated 1614 and copied from a stained-glass window in a cathedral at Berne, Switzerland, depicts pretzels used as the nuptial knot in a marriage ceremony between two royal families.

The knot-like shape of the pretzel became symbolic of the nuptial knot, and it often figured in the marriage ceremony. The wedding couple used it much like the wishbone is used now. The bride would link her finger in one loop, and the groom in the other. Silently each would make a wish then pull. Whoever came away with the larger piece was assured of getting his or her wish.

Traditional belief states that in 1620 the pretzel made its international debut in America when the Mayflower landed with the Pilgrims at Plymouth Rock. Where there were Pilgrims, there were Native Americans, and pretzels made great wampum.

In 1652 the earliest reference to pretzels in America appears in a story of the Hudson River by Carl Carmer. In his history of Beverwyck, New York, Carmer states that near Albany, Jochem Wessels and his wife, Gertrude, baked pretzels for the populace.

The Wessels were taken to court for selling pretzels to the Indians, who loved pretzels so much they would pay any price for them. The court case focused on the fact that the Wessels used good flour for the pretzels while they used remnants of the ground meal to bake bread for the citizenry. That is, the heathen were eating "good" flour while the Christians were eating bran flour. One must wonder if the townspeople knew of the pretzel's religious origin.

The Palantine Germans, later known as the Pennsylvania Dutch, also brought a pretzel tradition to America in 1710. German children wore pretzel necklaces on New Year's Day to symbolize good luck and prosperity for the coming year.

Rumor, Legend, and Reality

When did pretzels make their way to America? One rumor has it that the doughy knots came over on the Mayflower, and the Pilgrims used them for trade with Native Americans they met in the New World. One can daydream about what those settlers thought was important to pack and what all *did* actually come across the ocean in that vessel. Surely a freshly-baked pretzel wouldn't have withstood the length of the trip, but perhaps those early travelers brought the recipe and technique.

Early pretzels were soft inside and crusty on the outside, much like bread. In fact, they were made in bread bakeries as a specialty item. Legend has it that in the late 1800s, a hobo, possibly a European emigrant, passed through the town of Lititz, Pennsylvania, and stopped at the local bake shop to beg for a handout. In return, the tramp gave the baker his "secret recipe" for hard pretzels.

Before his death, Tom Sturgis, founder of Tom Sturgis Pretzels and grandson of Julius, founder of the first pretzel bakery in America, emphatically stated that the legend is HOGWASH.

Another legend claims hard pretzels were discovered when a lazy young baker's apprentice fell asleep on the job one day. His pretzels baked longer than usual, resulting in the crisp, tasty snack we all enjoy today.

All rumors and legends aside, REALITY is that in 1850 at the age of fifteen, Julius Sturgis worked in Lititz, Pennsylvania, at a bread bakery owned by Ambrose Rauch. As an apprentice baker, Julius had experience making soft pretzels. He noticed that occasionally pretzels or broken scraps of pretzels were left in the oven overnight and accidentally baked a second time, which made them hard and crispy.

So he began to experiment.

He discovered that if he rolled the dough thinner and smaller, those pretzels would bake faster, pack easier, and stay fresh longer. They also tasted good. So Julius approached Ambrose to see if he would allow him to make hard pretzels, a staple item to sell to general stores, but Ambrose said no.

Very business-minded and determined, Julius decided to open his own bakery in 1861. His little bakery became the very first commercial bakery in America that produced crispy, hard pretzels.

Julius Sturgis, His Home, and His Bakery

Julius Sturgis' family lived for a time in Jacksonville, Florida before migrating north to Pennsylvania some time during the early 1830s. Julius was born in Lititz, Pennsylvania on February 15, 1835. Julius made his first home as an independent adult in Lancaster, Pennsylvania, and worked as a gunsmith.

After moving to Lititz, Pennsylvania, Julius apprenticed for three years with a bread baker, Ambrose Rauch.

In 1861, Julius decided to abandon his apprenticeship with Rauch. He was determined to open his own bakery, dedicated to the baking of hard, crunchy pretzels. So at the young age of 26, he bought a stone house on the main street of Lititz, Pennsylvania, at 219 East Main Street, just down the street from Rauch's bake shop. He added space onto the back of the building to accommodate the pretzel business, and on May 9, 1861, that small shop at the rear of his family's home became the first commercial pretzel bakery in America.

When Julius purchased his home, it was already 77 years old, built in 1784 by Peter Kreiter and one of the original buildings in colonial Lititz. Builders dug the stones from the street out front and cut timber from surrounding forests.

Today when visiting Lititz, if you stand outside facing the front of the house, you can see the original builder's seal on the second floor above the front door. You'll see skinny barred basement windows at ground level on the sides of the building, built to allow the use of muskets when homeowners were defending their families against Native American attacks. The original plank-pegged, hardwood floors are visible in the entry hallway. The wood of the scrolled staircase bannister is original too. In some places, heavy wooden doors still hang on iron strap hinges. The front room on the left where tour tickets are purchased is part of the original house. The room directly behind it is now part of the museum but was originally part of the twisting room. To the rear of the twisting room, we see the original baking room and four pretzel ovens.

One thing is for sure—Julius' home saw a lot of activity. He ultimately had 14 children, and most of them were involved with the pretzel baking business through the years.

Additionally, through the years Julius offered room and board upstairs in his family's living quarters to some of his twisters and bakers. Along with her children, his wife usually fed up to ten bakery workers in the dining room of their home in those early days.

Julius operated the pretzel business there until he retired in 1893. After retiring, he enjoyed spending the winter months in Florida in his parents' former vacation home.

He died on October 4, 1897, at the age of 62.

Today the upstairs areas of his former bakery and home are utilized as rental apartments. One perk of living there is having the lovely smell of baking pretzels wafting up there each day.

The Julius Sturgis Pretzel House and Museum is listed on the National Register of Historic Places.

During the War Years

Julius Sturgis started his pretzel business in 1861. If you are good at history, you may be thinking about what was happening in our country in 1861. The year that Julius opened his pretzel bakery was also the year the American Civil War began.

Up until the start of the war, Lititz, Pennsylvania, was a town of booming industry with carriage makers, iron works, and other businesses lining Main Street and Broad Street. Even so, with the country suddenly focusing on the war effort, it must have been a difficult time for Julius to establish a new business.

Julius himself had "reserve" status during the war due to an injury he suffered after being kicked by a horse as a child. Even so, he was once called into active duty to help defend and later burn the bridge at Columbia. This defense caused the Confederate troops to march toward the battle of Gettysburg in 1863.

After a few years in business, Julius was almost ready to throw in the towel because he couldn't pay his bills. (Stores then normally only settled their accounts once every six years.) However, word of his financial troubles must have spread, and a big store owner from Columbia offered to pay the account in advance so that Julius could stay in business. The Columbian retailer said he needed the pretzels to satisfy the demands of his customers. The bill, for about $300, gave Julius the funds and the incentive to stay in business.

Julius' strong business sense allowed him to build his business through the war years, which was probably due as much to his abilities as a marketer as to his skills as a baker.

Just fifteen years after starting his business, Julius had his pretzel registered as "THE ONLY GENUINE LITITZ BRETZELS," which indicates his product had achieved significant fame throughout the region.

Julius' success also spurred other bakers to go into the business, with pretzel bakeries in Lititz at one time numbering up to thirteen.

From 1861 to the present, the Sturgis family has operated in continuous pretzel production with the exception of two years during World War II when bakery employees were drafted into military service. Today Sturgis descendants into the sixth generation are active in various areas of the pretzel baking business.

BAKING PRETZELS, THEN AND NOW

Baking in the Olden Days (According to the Baker)

...Hard work, long hours, mixing, kneading, twisting, sweating, pretzels! All in a day's work for the Master Baker and the Baker's Apprentice....

If we could go back in history and visit an early pretzel bakery, here's what the Master Baker might have to say:

"Our workday starts quite early; while it's still dark we arrive at the bakery to begin the early morning dough-mixing. As the Master Baker, I am the one to combine the proper proportions of ingredients. Meanwhile, my apprentice starts the fires under our cooking pot and the oven hearth.

"After mixing and kneading the dough, I cut it into small lumps. Each lump is rolled into a long, thin strip. Then, with a quick flick of my wrists, I twist a pretzel. There is no time to lose now; day is starting to dawn, and of course, a slow pretzel twister will never get the job finished on time.

"Next, the pretzels are placed into the cooking pot containing a bubbling solution of straw water. When the dough is cooked, my helper ladles the pretzels out of the cooker, places them onto his long-handled peel, sprinkles them with salt, and slides them onto the oven hearth to bake. The peel for loading the pretzels into the oven resembles the tool pizza-bakers use, except that it's long and narrow to slide one long row of pretzels carefully onto the oven hearth.

"By now, there's quite a lot happening in our little bakery with all the dough-mixing, twisting, cooking, fire-tending, salting, and baking going on continuously. I must always keep one eye on my apprentice—more than once he burned the pretzels. Then there's that little Dutch boy, always around here somewhere hoping for a handout.

"When the pretzels are baked, my helper uses a peel to carefully remove them from the oven. This peel is wider than the other one and has thin edges so it can scoop many pretzels out of the oven swiftly. Gently we stack them onto wooden trays with wire mesh bottoms. Since the attic is much warmer by now, we take the pretzels up there to dry until they are crisp and crunchy. In several hours we will carry them down again to be packed into barrels or sold over the counter.

"Later, if time and pretzels remain, my apprentice fills some baskets with fresh pretzels and goes down the lane into the village or over to the next farmhouse. Folks are usually glad to buy our tasty snacks.

"Finally, at the end of a long day, we clean up the shop and head for home. As for the few remaining pretzels, our families will eagerly devour them. While I glance back at my tired helper, I tell myself that someday I must figure out a more efficient way of doing all this and still keep the good taste…"

Baking Pretzels in the 19th Century

The Ingredients

In the early days of pretzel making, pretzel dough only consisted of flour, water, and yeast. Of course, we need dough to make pretzels. The raw ingredients and the implements for mixing the dough were all stored and used on the one side of the twisting room in Julius' little bakery.

Flour would be delivered to the bakery and hauled in sacks to the second level of the home. From there it would be dumped through the flour chute to the first floor where the flour would be added into the dough mix.

One of the first and most important steps in pretzel baking was making good yeast. Quality yeast created fermentation in the dough and produced a crispy, crunchy pretzel.

Mixing the Dough

The three ingredients would be combined into a large mixer, a large wooden barrel, until the dough held together in a large mass.

Next the dough would be removed from the mixer and plopped down onto the dough break, a quarter oak with a jumping rail. To picture a dough break, imagine one quarter of a circular table built into the corner of a room. The dough would be placed on the dough break. One of the bakers or twisters would sit on the dough break lever—the jumping rail—and jump the lever up, down, and back and forth over the pile of dough. The massive mounds of dough required this large piece of equipment and the strength of a man to adequately knead them.

After it was kneaded, the dough was placed into the dough trays to rise.

Finally, one of the pretzel twisters brought the risen dough to the twisting table.

Twisting the Pretzels
In the twisting area, one of the twisters would cut the large mass

Lewis Sturgis

of dough into small pieces, each enough to form one pretzel, and place them on the twisting table. The twisting table was long and narrow and contained shallow grooves running lengthwise that were helpful when rolling the small lumps of dough into long strips.

Approximately ten to fifteen pretzel twisters, both men and women, would commence twisting. First, the small lump of dough was rolled into a long strip. The twister picked up the strip by both ends, gave a quick flick of the wrists, and shaped the dough into the well-known pretzel shape.

A few of the most legendary twisters were able to twist up to forty pretzels per minute but only if the lumps of dough were already rolled into strips and ready to twist. (Today Helen Hoff holds the world championship record for pretzel twisting. She twisted fifty-seven pretzels per minute.)[1]

In Julius' bakery, twisters were expected to work about sixty hours a week at $.10 an hour, which would earn them a weekly pay amount of $6.00. They received $3 in cash and $3 in credit to spend at other businesses in town.

---

[1] J & J Snack Foods Corporation; "Superpretzel Honors Twisted Snack During Natinal Soft Pretzel Month," April 1, 2015, www.prnewswire.com.

Preparing to Bake the Pretzels

Once the pretzels had been twisted, they were placed on boards to "proof" or rise.

After a while, the bakers would dip them into a solution of straw water and lye. This process gave the pretzels their shiny brown color and flavor. After dipping them, they would arrange the wet pretzels on a muslin-covered box known as a couch board so the excess liquid would drain off.

Baking the Pretzels

Julius kept his four ovens heated to 550 degrees, fired by wood, coal, or sometimes coke—whatever was most readily available.

The bakers took the pretzels out of the couch board one by one and placed them onto a peel, a long-handled tool used to load the pretzels into the oven. It resembles our modern pizza-baking tool but is narrower.

After salting the pretzels, the baker used the peel to load row after row of pretzels into the oven. After about ten minutes in the 550-degree ovens, the pretzels were fully baked and ready to be removed from the oven.

Four brick ovens, ten-hour days, six days a week. Lots of pretzels came out of Julius' little bakery.

Drying the Pretzels

When the pretzels were done baking, bakers used the peel again to remove them from the oven and drop them into wire mesh trays. When the trays were full, they were loaded onto shelves in a wooden elevator.

This elevator was hoisted up to the second floor where the heat rising from all four ovens would essentially bake the pretzels a second time. This second baking is called the drying, since it removes any remaining moisture and turns them into hard, crispy pretzels.

The upstairs drying rooms would have been between 150 and 250 degrees and the pretzels could take anywhere from two hours to two days to dry depending on the season and the humidity levels.

Packaging and Selling the Pretzels

When the pretzels were finished drying, they were ready for packing and selling. These hard pretzels quickly grew in popularity as a snack food since they stayed fresh much longer than soft pretzels when kept in an airtight container.

Some of the pretzels were sold right there at the bakery to walk-in customers. The majority of the pretzels were packed in barrels to be shipped and sold. Horses and wagons carried them to their final destinations on the grocery store shelves.

If there were left-over pretzels but not enough to fill a barrel, they were placed into baskets. One of the bakery employees would load several baskets into the wagon and peddle them down the lane and around the community.

Baking Pretzels in the 20th Century

By 1900, most bakeries fired the ovens with coal or coke, and with the passage of time came the advances of growing technology in all areas of pretzel production.

By 1910, automation came into the pretzel bakeries. First there were engine-powered dough breakers or kneaders that removed much of the drudgery and heavy work from mixing.

Next came the pretzel-rolling machine. That machine cut a lump of the proper size for one pretzel and rolled the dough into strips. A canvas belt fed the strips to line workers who twisted them into the pretzel shape and placed them on trays. Many twisters became fast and skillful, shaping up to 40 per minute. At that time, most pretzel people said there would never be a machine built to twist pretzels.

Until the 1930s, pretzels were still manufactured by hand. Then in 1933, the Reading Pretzel Machinery Company introduced the first automated pretzel twister, which enabled bakers to produce about 50-120 pretzels per minute depending on the pretzel type and consistency of the dough, which easily exceeded the maximum 40 per minute an individual worker could make by hand.

These early pretzel-twisting machines had a vertical mechanism consisting of many parts and could only twist the regular thin pretzels. Meanwhile, engineers were already working on other twisting machines that would be capable of making the thicker, crunchier pretzels. In the 1950's American Machine & Foundry (AMF) developed this newer version of the pretzel-twisting machine. Its mechanical fingers tie dough rods into raw pretzels before dropping them down onto the conveyor belt. The production capacity of one AMF pretzel-tying unit is 50 pretzels per minute or 24,000 per eight-hour baking shift.

By 1950, many pretzel factories had incorporated either the Reading Pretzel Machinery or the AMF twisting machines into their production lines. That technological marvel increased the average worker's output from 25 pounds per hour to 150 pounds per hour—a six-fold increase in productivity.

Next came larger dough mixers, and rotary hearth ovens gave way to tunnel ovens at least 50 feet in length.

The head baker added the pretzel dough ingredients into a large automatic dough mixer. When the dough was mixed, the baker opened the mixer door and guided the large mass of dough out onto a rolling cutting table. Using a large knife, he slashed manageable

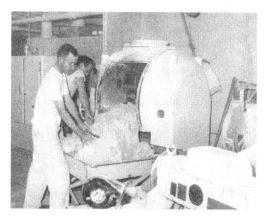

portions of dough from the batch and hoisted the portions up into each of the twisting machine hoppers.

As the dough pressed down through the hopper and out a small hole at the bottom, a sharp rotating blade cut off another small amount of dough. This small lump traveled through two moving conveyors. By moving in opposite directions, the conveyors rolled the lump of dough into a long skinny strip and dropped it into a trough.

At the bottom of the rolling conveyors, two pinchers grabbed the ends of the dough strip and robotically twisted it into the shape of a pretzel. The platform on which the pretzel was twisted then flipped over, dropping the pretzel onto a moving conveyor belt toward the oven.

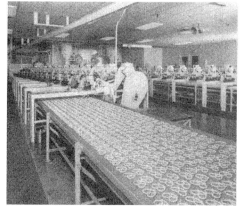

Because the hoppers and twisting machines were staggered in their placement along the belt, many pretzels traveled at once toward the oven. The baker's helper had the job of watching the twisting machines for jam-ups, manually removing any defectively-twisted pretzels from the belt, and re-twisting them by hand.

However, by the mid-1950s, as the pretzel industry continued to grow, even the automatic pretzel twister soon became inadequate to meet manufacturers' needs. Looming on the horizon was a new process for forming pretzels—high-speed extrusion.

A pretzel extruder could be described as a large, stainless steel version of a child's play dough toy. Dough is forced through a die that forms the pretzels' shapes. A long blade cuts off 14 pretzels with one stroke. By the 1960s, extrusion technology in the pretzel industry became common.

As the pretzels moved on the belt toward the ovens, the dough had time to rise a bit before baking. The dough rising process is called proofing. Prior to baking, the pretzels passed through a soda bath. This bath gave the pretzels their burnished brown color and sheen and provided a way for the salt to stick.

After the pretzels were salted, they were baked and then traveled by conveyor into the dryer, where they essentially got a second baking.

From the dryer a conveyor carried the pretzels into the packing room. In the first half of the twentieth century, packers stood along the line with scoops and hand shovels. They hand-weighed and packaged the pretzels into bags, cartons, and tins.

Toward the last quarter of the twentieth century, all pretzel manufacturers incorporated many forms of computerized machinery, including dough mixers, scales, and packaging machines. Already the pretzel-making process has evolved much from its early days.

Baking Pretzels in the 21st Century

Out of Julius Sturgis' one small bakery in Lititz grew the pretzel industry as we know it today. As the change from hand twisting to automatic twisting to extrusion, all modernizations we see in this century will be for enhanced and increased productivity.

Most modern pretzel bakeries are fully automated and computerized with numerous safety checkpoints in place. And they all continue experimenting and expanding their offerings to include new shapes and flavors of pretzels.

In the nineteenth century bakers had one offering—the traditional pretzel. In the twentieth century, pretzel shapes evolved, and flavors expanded. Continuing in the twenty-first century, we should expect to see the creation of more complex pretzel shapes and a wider variety of seasonings and flavors such as the Soy pretzel, which is becoming a favorite of the health-conscious snacker.

As in any of the other food industries, governmental agencies require a multitude of checkpoints and inspection regimens. The FDA (Food and Drug Administration) is responsible for regulating and placing a nutrition facts label on all processed foods created and sold in the United States. OSHA (the Occupational Safety and

Health Administration) makes regulations for the production plant with the safety of employees and customers in mind. Kosher certified pretzels require regular plant inspections. Metal detectors on the production lines protect consumers from accidental product contamination or purposeful sabotage.

With all that regulation, today's pretzel bakery personnel spend more and more time each year completing required documentation and other agency-required paperwork.

Concerning marketing, social media has become a big plus. Most pretzel bakeries have professional websites with online stores. Most also have extensive and influential online presence and managers to oversee their Facebook, Instagram, Twitter, and other internet accounts.

Although pretzel machinery has changed a great deal since the infancy of the pretzel industry, at Tom Sturgis Pretzels, Inc., one thing has not changed—pretzels are still baked on a soapstone hearth surface. These soapstone hearths, made in Vermont, retain the heat more evenly than wire racks.

Keeping the stone baking surface while modernizing in other aspects of pretzel production epitomizes our effort to retain the features of baking which make the highest quality pretzels available.

The Packaging Process

Today, computerized weighing and bagging machines do the work, although a designated packing room at the production facility is still filled with workers who hand-pack the bags into boxes and prepare the cartons for shipping. From there most pretzels are sent to distribution sites within a 150-mile radius. As of this printing, Tom Sturgis distributes pretzels wholesale to farmers' markets and grocery stores in nine states: Pennsylvania, New Jersey, Delaware, Maryland, Virginia, West Virginia, New York, Wisconsin, and Texas. (As always, the sales team works to expand the market range.)

The Basic Pretzel Making Process Today

The methods of producing food, especially pretzels, have changed dramatically over the last hundred or so years. In a modern, fully automated pretzel bakery, pretzels are produced as follows:

1. **Dough mixing:** The production process begins with the mixing of ingredients according to the baker's formula. Ingredients are mixed together, 300 pounds at a time, forming a rather stiff dough.

2. **Extrusion:** The dough is put into machines that extrude it into various pretzel shapes, depending on what type of pretzels is being made that day.

3. **Dough Rises:** Pretzel shapes are dropped onto a conveyor belt which carries them 125 feet to the cooker. This "ride" gives the dough sufficient time to rise before the next phase.

4. **Cooking:** The pretzels pass through the cooker. The cooker contains caustic soda and water. This mixture makes the pretzels shiny and brown when they are baked.

5. **Salting:** Salt is dropped onto the pretzels while they are wet from the cooking solution.

6. **Baking:** After salting, pretzels enter the oven for baking. They are baked at temperatures exceeding 500 degrees. (Most baked foods such as bread and cookies are baked at lower temps.) Tom Sturgis Pretzels uses stone hearth ovens. Large slabs of soapstone attached to conveyors move the pretzels through the ovens.

7. **Drying:** From the oven, pretzels go on conveyor belts to the dryer to have the moisture removed so that they are crispy and crunchy.

8. **Packing:** Computerized packing machines form the bags, weigh the correct number of pretzels, fill the bags, and seal them.

9. **Shipping:** Pretzel bags are put into cartons (still by hand) and shipped by trucks to stores for display and sale.
10. **Other sales:** Pretzels are sold both in the local Tom Sturgis retail store at the manufacturing factory and through internet purchases.

THE PRETZEL

The Classic Pretzel Shape

If you're any sort of a pretzel connoisseur, you're well familiar with the iconic pretzel shape. Both the Tom Sturgis Pretzels factory and the Julius Sturgis Pretzel House have gargantuan pretzel statues in front of their factories to welcome visitors and provide fun photo opportunities.

Most pretzels have that signature shape that resembles a knot. The pretzel's unique shape is a symmetrical loop created by intertwining the ends of a long strip of dough then folding them back on each other, forming a "pretzel loop."

But where did this shape come from? What does it mean, if anything? Was it a random twist of the dough?

Probably not. We do know of numerous stories and traditions—all likely contributing at some point in some way to explaining the traditional shape of the pretzel.

Yes, it is possible that each step of the pretzel twisting process had significance.

Remember, centuries ago, the children were treated with these little baked goodies if they learned to say their prayers well. If the strip of dough is first shaped into a "U," this represents the children's prayers going up to heaven.

Next the ends of the "U" are crossed are crossed over to form an "X" and then twisted one time. Perhaps the resulting knot represented the union of marriage between the children's parents. Some wonder if the pretzel gave us the marriage phrase of "tying the knot."

For some, the interlocking loops of the pretzel symbolize undying love, and pretzels, therefore, were a symbolic part of wedding ceremonies in years past. Sometimes the couple would make a wish. The bride and groom would each hold a side of the pretzel, much like our custom of pulling the turkey wishbone. Each would try to break off the biggest piece so their wish would come true. Since they were both wishing for happiness, they both always won!

Finally, the ends of the dough are pulled down and pressed onto the bottom of the pretzel, creating three holes in the shape. Some say these three holes represent the trinity in the Christian faith—the Father, Son, and Holy Spirit.

How to Twist a Pretzel

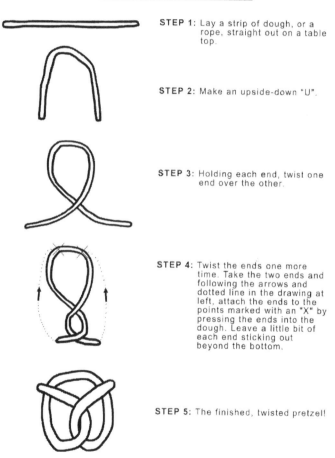

STEP 1: Lay a strip of dough, or a rope, straight out on a table top.

STEP 2: Make an upside-down "U".

STEP 3: Holding each end, twist one end over the other.

STEP 4: Twist the ends one more time. Take the two ends and following the arrows and dotted line in the drawing at left, attach the ends to the points marked with an "X" by pressing the ends into the dough. Leave a little bit of each end sticking out beyond the bottom.

STEP 5: The finished, twisted pretzel!

Pretzel Ingredients—Then and Now

Bakers needed to know how to make quality yeast. Yeast creates fermentation in the dough and produces a crispy, crunchy pretzel.

In the early days of pretzel baking, pretzel dough only contained three ingredients—flour, water, and yeast. These ingredients were mixed in large wooden barrels.

Surely Julius Sturgis would be astonished today if he were to see the warehouse and refrigeration areas needed to store the ingredients for modern pretzel baking. The large tanks of flour that Sturgis Pretzels gets by the truckload and the computerized automation of those flour silos that receive, contain, and dispense the flour would put him in awe too.

As expected, each pretzel bakery has its own set of recipes for combining these ingredients. Specialty flavored pretzels use additional ingredients—cheese and cheese flavoring, soy, sesame seeds, chocolate, ranch seasoning, barbeque flavoring, and many others. For those consumers watching their sodium intake, some pretzels are baked without any surface salt.

Today, the principal ingredients in Tom Sturgis Pretzels are local winter wheat flour, shortening, yeast, malt syrup, soda, salt, and water. Each pretzel variety has its own recipe using these basic ingredients in different proportions.

The Sturgis family's determination to use only the best ingredients along with traditional Sturgis baking methods helps produce the present top-quality Tom Sturgis pretzels.

Pretzels – A Nutritious Snack

Besides being a tasty snack that the whole family can enjoy, pretzels are a surprisingly healthy food. They contain no empty calories, no fat (except for cheese pretzels or other seasoned varieties), and no chemical additives or preservatives.

Made of simple ingredients, pretzels have only 110 calories per one ounce serving, converting to six to eight small hard pretzels. True "pretzelmaniacs" don't care about the calorie count, the sodium content (465 milligrams/serving), or the carbohydrates (21 grams/serving). Instead, they worry if a snack stand, pub, or supermarket is going to be handy when the craving hits.

Made from wheat flour, pretzels are an appropriate snack for most people to eat at any hour of the day without fear of discomfort.

Pretzels are a concentrated food, rich in protein and also containing calcium, phosphate, and other mineral elements. Some manufacturers use enriched flour in their pretzels. Others add protein, calcium, and iron, thus making the pretzel a completely nutritious food.

The crispness of pretzels exercises the teeth, and the salt helps to replace that lost by the body when exposed to heat.

Pretzels often provide the answer to a mother's problem of children begging for between meal snacks. Additionally, they serve well with soups, cheese, salads, seafoods, hot and cold beverages, and ice cream.

Many mothers use pretzels for their babies as teethers. In fact, for many years one well-known baby item manufacturer produced pink, blue, and yellow hard rubber teethers in the shape of the traditional pretzel. Children fill one of the largest consumer segments of this universal product.

Pretzel Varieties

Today pretzels are manufactured in a wide variety of shapes, sizes, and flavors.

As this book goes to print, Tom Sturgis Pretzels offers the varieties of pretzels and pretzel snacks listed below. As always, our bakers and masterminds are actively researching new pretzel flavors and pretzel products as you read this.

Traditional Styles:
(the larger-sized pretzels)
Specials
Dutch Style
Cheese

Variations on the larger-sized pretzels:
Thins
Low Sodium
Crunchzels
Sourdough Hard

Mini Pretzels:
Little Ones
Low Sodium Little Ones
Little Cheesers
Hot Cheesers
Low Sodium Little Cheesers
Jalapeno Minis
Soy Pretzel Nuggets

Nontraditionally-shaped Pretzels:
Horse and Buggy Pretzels
Chris B's Pretzels

Stick Pretzels:
Thick Stiks
Thin Stiks
Chocolate Cookie Stiks
Honey Graham Stiks
Cinnamon Sugar Stiks

Snack Pretzels:
Regular Gems
Cheese Gems
Peanut Butter-Filled Nuggets

Pretzel Bits:
Honey Mustard and Onion Pretzel Bits
Ranch Pretzel Bits
Barbeque Pretzel Bits

Chocolate Pretzels:
Milk and Dark Chocolate Covered Specials
Chocolate Covered Little Ones
Chocolate Covered Crunchzels
Chocolate Covered Stiks
Milk or Dark Chocolate Covered Crunchzel Bits
Pretzel Raisin Chocolate Bark
Milk or Dark Chocolate Peanut Butter Little Ones

Milk or Dark Chocolate Caramel Little Ones
Chocolate Covered Pretzel Peanut Brittle Bites
Chocolate Covered Horse and Buggy Pretzels
Milk and Dark Chocolate Covered Cinnamon Sugar Stiks
Milk and Dark Chocolate Covered Honey Graham Stiks

Miscellaneous:
Soft Pretzel Mix
Pretzel Crumbs

(Are you hungry for a pretzel yet?)

OTHER INTERESTING PRETZEL FACTS

How Many Pretzels?

Over $1.3 billion worth of pretzels are sold in the United States annually.[2] That translates into a total production of over 300 million pounds of pretzels and pretzel products. Eighty percent are made in Pennsylvania, where hard pretzels originated.

For comparison, total snack food sales are about $23 billion a year in the United States.

The average United States citizen consumes up to two pounds of pretzels per year. Pennsylvanians have the highest per capita consumption in the country, with Philadelphians snacking on about twelve pounds of pretzels per person per year.

The pretzel market in general has grown in recent years because pretzels are considered to be a healthier, fat-free snack than many other snacks.

Tom Sturgis Pretzels acquires about $6 million in yearly pretzel sales, equal to about five million pounds of pretzels annually.

The Pretzel City of the World

Many folks say Reading, Pennsylvania, is the Pretzel City of the World. To be sure, quite a lot of the history of pretzels has happened in the city of Reading. Take a look at the evolution of pretzel making through the years and its arrival in Reading:

610: The pretzel was invented.

1861: Julius Sturgis opens the first commercial pretzel bakery in Lititz, Pennsylvania.

1864: J. S. Bachman founds Bachman Pretzels on North 11th Street in Reading, Pennsylvania.

1860s (later): Benjamin Lichtenthaler founds a pretzel bakery on Apple Street in Reading, Pennsylvania.

1911: Edward J. Faller founds E. J. Faller Pretzel Company in Reading, Pennsylvania.

---

[2] Miller, Jeffrey. "How the Pretzel Went from Soft to Hard—and Other Little-Known Facts About One of the World's Favorite Snacks." *The Conversation*. Retrieved April 26, 2018.

1921: The Spannuth family founds Unique Pretzel Bakery in Muhlenburg Township, Reading, Pennsylvania.

1931: William R. Edmundson founds Billy's Butter Bretzels on Plum Street in Reading, Pennsylvania.

1945: Joe Dmochowski founds Reading Hard and Soft Pretzel Bakery (also known as Bell Alley Soft Pretzels).

1946: Marriott "Tom" Sturgis (grandson of Julius Sturgis) founds Tom Sturgis Pretzels on Grape Street in Reading, Pennsylvania.

2012: Bachman brand pretzels' rights are sold to Utz, and Savor Street Foods is founded.

At one time there were 25-30 pretzel bakeries in Reading, Pennsylvania alone. It's no wonder that people considered it (Some still do) to be the pretzel capital of the world.

Notably, the key to the city of Reading has a pretzel on it.

National Pretzel Day

In the United States, pretzel connoisseurs celebrate National Pretzel Day each year on April 26. The idea of having a National Pretzel Day originated in the mind of Robert Walker, a Lancaster County man.

In 1983, the U.S. Representative Walker (Republican, PA) introduced Pretzel Day to the Congress as a means of recognizing the invaluable contributions of the numerous pretzel bakeries within the state and their impact on the nation's economy.

In 2003, PA Governor Ed Rendell declared April 26th to be National Pretzel Day each year to acknowledge the importance of the pretzel to the state's history and economy.

With a little creativity, one can enjoy celebrating this unique holiday each year. Following are a few fun ideas to get you and your family started enjoying National Pretzel Day:

- Mark the date on your calendar so you don't miss it!
- Bake some soft pretzels and serve warm with mustard. Use the recipe in this book.
- Take a tour of one of the local pretzel bakeries.
- Visit the Julius Sturgis Pretzel House and Museum in Lititz, PA, where it all started.
- Try making a new pretzel recipe for your family's enjoyment.

- After dinner, have two family members break a pretzel and make a wish, similar to the breaking of the turkey wishbone.
- Explore Pinterest and find a fun pretzel craft to do with your kids or grandkids.
- Slather up a large pretzel with peanut butter and birdseed. Hang it out in your yard for the birds.
- Eat some ice cream with pretzel crumbs sprinkled on top.
- Purchase a variety of pretzels to try that you've never tasted before.

<u>Pretzel Trivia</u>

- Helen Hoft is the world champion pretzel twister. She could twist 57 pretzels per minute, as long as the dough strips were ready for her to grab.
- The largest known pretzel in the world weighed in at 842 pounds. It measured 26.8 feet long and 10.2 feet high.
- Pretzels without salt are called "baldies."
- The two ends of the strip of dough in a formed pretzel are called "baby eye pokers."
- Tom Sturgis Pretzels employs 30 employees and produces over five million pounds of pretzels annually.
- Pretzel extruders push out over 1900 pretzels per minute.
- Some of Tom Sturgis's pretzels appeared in the movie "For Richer or Poorer." Stars included Tim Allen and Kirstie Alley. The pretzels appeared in a scene set in a general store.
- The average American eats two pounds of pretzels a year.
- The average Pennsylvanian eats 25 pounds of pretzels a year.
- A gilded-edge pretzel hanging over a door in Germany or Switzerland designates the establishment as a baker's shop.
- One band of musicians that played around Lititz in the early 1900s named themselves the Pretzelets.
- Each year since 1951 a benefit football game—the Pretzel Bowl—has been played, featuring a pretzel-decorated trophy, a parade with pretzel floats, and, of course, a pretzel queen.
- The mascot for the Tom Sturgis Pretzel Company is the Little Dutch Boy. The pretzel out in front of the Tom Sturgis Pretzels

factory is about ten feet long by eight feet high. When it was installed in 1973 it cost about $3500.

Presidents, Politicians, and Pretzels

A few ardent pretzel historians believe that a yearning for freshly-baked pretzels stirred up such hunger in the soul of our only bachelor president, James Buchanan, that in 1861 when a constituent back home in PA Dutch Country set up a pretzel factory, Buchanan gave up the White House to hustle back to where the pretzels were.

Pretzels had such an extravagant hold on Buchanan that half the populace was irked to a frenzy. Civil War ensued.

In 1958, a Pennsylvanian, Arthur McGonigle, sold his Bachman Pretzel Company that he'd bought during the Great Depression. A pretzel maker turned politician, he campaigned for governor using the slogan "a new twist in government—clean, honest, efficient." He lost the election, no doubt voters' retribution for selling his pretzel company to a snuff maker.

Pretzel proponents can be tolerant. That is, they love political losers as much as they thrill to the winners. They treated then-Presidential hopeful to a consolation party topped by robust soft pretzels made by the Federal Baking Company, Inc. Later, in May they honored President Ronald Reagan at a party, again highlighted by their favorite snack—pretzels.

President George W. Bush was munching on a pretzel in the White House when he choked and lost consciousness while watching the 2002 Baltimore-Miami NFL playoff game. In recalling the incident, he urges, "When you're eating pretzels, chew before you swallow. Listen to your mother." (From Bush Press Conference, YouTube. Retrieved 7 February 2012.)

RECIPES

Favorite Pretzel Recipes

Pretzel Stuffing

(For stuffing a chicken, use recipe as is.
For stuffing a turkey, triple the recipe.)

Ingredients:
3 cups pretzel crumbs, fine or medium (9 to 12 ounces of pretzels)
1/2 cup chopped onion
1/2 cup butter
3/4 cup diced celery
1/2 teaspoon poultry seasoning
1/4 teaspoon ground sage
1/8 teaspoon ground pepper
1 1/3 cups chicken stock or bouillon

Directions:
Crush pretzels by placing in a Ziploc bag and rolling with rolling pin.
Sauté onion in butter until soft, but not browned.
Meanwhile blend celery, seasonings, and crumbs.
To crumb mixture, add stock or bouillon and sautéed onion with the butter.
Toss with fork to blend ingredients.
If desired add more seasoning.
The addition of salt depends on saltiness of pretzels and stock or bouillon.
Makes 4 to 4 1/2 cups pretzel stuffing—enough for body and wishbone cavities of a 4 to 5 pound ready-to-cook chicken.

Famous Pennsylvania Pretzel Soup

Ingredients:
2 or more pretzels
Boiling water
1/2 teaspoon butter
1 cup hot milk
Salt and pepper, to taste

Directions:
Break pretzels into a small deep dish.
Add boiling water to cover and steep, covered, for about a minute.
Pour off water then add butter and hot milk. Season and serve.
Serves one.

Soft Pretzels

Ingredients:
1 package of dry yeast
1 1/2 cups warm water
1 tablespoon sugar
4 cups flour
1 beaten egg
Coarse kosher salt

Directions:
Dissolve the yeast in water. Then add the sugar and salt.
Blend in the flour and turn the dough onto a lightly floured surface.
Knead until smooth. Cut off slices of the dough and roll them into
ropes. Twist the ropes into pretzel shapes and arrange them on a
cookie sheet lined with greased brown paper.
Brush the pretzels with the egg. Sprinkle coarse salt on them.
Bake at 425 degrees for 12 to 15 minutes or until golden brown.

Pretzel Sculpture Craft

Supplies:
Thin pretzel sticks
Small and large marshmallows

Directions:
Stick the pretzel sticks into marshmallows to create a 3-dimensional sculpture.
Eat the sculpture!

Sturgis Family's Favorite Pretzel Recipes

Ranch Pretzel Bits

Ingredients:
2 pounds sourdough hard pretzels
2 pounds other pretzels
1 package ranch dressing mix (dry powder)
1 cup vegetable oil
1/2 teaspoon lemon pepper
1/2 teaspoon garlic powder
1/2 teaspoon dill weed

Directions:
Break or smash pretzels into bite-sized pieces.
Pour pretzels into baking pans. You will probably need two rectangular cake pans.
Mix all ingredients together and pour over pretzels. Stir until pretzels are completely coated. Leave sit for about an hour allowing flavors to soak in and then preheat oven to 350 degrees.
Bake for about 20 minutes, stirring once or twice.
Allow to cool and store in airtight containers.

Strawberry Pretzel Dessert

Ingredients:
1 1/2 cups crushed pretzels
1 stick margarine, melted
1/4 cup sugar
1 – 8-ounce package cream cheese
3/4 cup sugar
2 cups whipped topping
2 – 3-ounce packages strawberry Jell-O
2 – 10-ounce packages frozen sliced strawberries
2 cups boiling water

Directions:
Mix pretzels, margarine and sugar. Press in a 9 x 13-inch pan.
Bake at 375 degrees for 10 minutes.
Blend cream cheese and sugar, then beat in whipped topping and mix well. Put on top of cooled crust.
Dissolve packages of Jell-O in 2 cups boiling water.
Add frozen strawberries. (Do not thaw them.)
When this starts to set, put on top of creamed mixture.
Refrigerate until serving time.

Variation: May use raspberries in place of strawberries.

No-Bake Party Mix

Ingredients:
8 cups Crispix cereal
2 1/2 cups mini pretzel sticks
2 1/2 cups mini cheddar cheese crackers
3 tablespoons vegetable oil
1 package ranch salad dressing mix (dry powder)

Directions:
In a heavy 2-gallon Ziploc bag, combine cereal, pretzels and crackers.
Drizzle with oil.
Seal and gently toss.
Sprinkle with dressing mix.
Seal and toss again.
Store in an airtight container.

Chocolate Pretzel Kisses

Ingredients:
Miniature pretzels
Hershey's kisses
M & M's

Directions:
Arrange miniature pretzels on ungreased cookie tray.
Place unwrapped Hershey's kisses on top of each pretzel.
Put tray in a preheated oven at 250 degrees for 5 minutes.
Take out and immediately push one M & M into top of softened kiss. Cool.

Recipe for a Successful Pretzel Making Business

Combine:
People:
Loyal, hard-working employees
A strong work ethic
Ability to address changing food trends
Flexible managers who are willing to wear many hats,
from baker to administrator

Critical Ingredients:
Good local water supply
Soft red winter wheat grown in the area

Processes:
Hourly hands on, in mouth quality testing
Regular upgrade of technology and machinery
Extra time for pretzels to proof on conveyor belts for
flavor
Creation of low-carb, high-protein, high-fiber pretzels
for the medical and nutrition markets
Adding new flavor lines to keep customer interest

Other:
Keep the product versatile.
Never sacrifice quality for quantity.
Keep the old methods that still produce quality today.
Toss in a bit of luck.
Appreciate loyalty of consumers.

FROM THE STURGIS FAMILY

Quotes from the Early Years of Pretzel Baking

Tom Sturgis tells of a memory from his late teenage days. His father, Marriott, picked him up to drive to work together one day.

"I don't like your attitude," Marriott said. He spit a bit of chewing tobacco, and one tiny speck of it landed on the windshield.

He pointed to it, and said, "This is what you know. The rest of the windshield is what you don't know."

Two years before his death in August of 1999, Marriott (Tom) Sturgis, grandson of Julius Sturgis and the original founder in 1946 of Tom Sturgis Pretzels, shared some things he learned from his many years of pretzel baking.

"One thing I've noticed since I was a little boy: There are some men that have the feel and touch to become a baker. To operate a business, you must have some know-how."

And on baking excellent pretzels, he said this: "The quality is good … if you gobble five at a sitting instead of two."

Commenting on the hard years early in his business he said, "I learned that you better use your mind."

Wise advice for anyone at any stage of business and life, to be sure.

A Last Interview

Shortly before his death in 1999, Marriott ("Tom") Sturgis reminisced at a family gathering. He left us with these words:

"Let's for once and for all get the Julius Sturgis Pretzel Story correct and accurate. I might be considered an expert about this. He was my grandfather. My mother and father worked for him.

"For the past thirty years I have read so much legend, hokum, and bunk on the origin of the first commercial pretzel bakery in the United States that I need to tell it like it was.

"Every time the Julius Sturgis Pretzels Story is printed, it says 'generally recognized,' or 'probably,' or 'most likely' he started the first commercial pretzel bakery in the United States. The facts are Julius Sturgis not only started the first commercial pretzel bakery in the United States, he also developed and perfected the first hard, crispy pretzel that we know today.

"Some legends say Julius Sturgis was born in Florida and wandered into Lititz, Pennsylvania as a young man. Bunk! Julius was born on February 15, 1835, in Lititz, Pennsylvania. The Moravian Church archives have this information recorded.

"Other stories say a tramp passing through Lititz gave Ambrose Rauch a recipe for hard pretzels. Somehow Julius, his apprentice, got his hands on this. This is pure hokum and never did happen.

"My mother and father, also my great uncle Edwin Sturgis, who passed away many years ago, told me when I was a little boy how the Julius Sturgis Pretzel Bakery started. They were *there* and didn't go for anything but the truth.

"The accounts and stories of pretzels being sold on the streets of Pennsylvania Dutch towns in the early nineteenth century are correct. Every German baker knew how to make lye pretzels. Today, we call them soft pretzels. In Berks County, they were called fresh pretzels. They had to be eaten the same day they were baked.

"Ambrose Rauch owned and operated a general bakery in Lititz, Pennsylvania. The primary products were bread, buns, rolls, etc. Julius Sturgis was an apprentice baker in the Rauch bakery. They baked a few soft pretzels as favors to housewives and kiddies. In the larger towns, soft pretzels were a side line in the general bakeries. They were sold on the streets by peddlers. Due to weather, rain, and snow they were considered an undependable product.

"The hard, crispy pretzels were an accident, waiting to be developed. It would happen occasionally that a few soft pretzels were left on the oven plate overnight, or a few left in the oven as a batch was finished. These were dried out. The bakers and their families enjoyed these crispy, hard pretzels.

"Julius Sturgis knew from experimenting that the pretzels could be kept in good crispy condition for two or three weeks by carefully wrapping them in butcher's paper.

He developed a very mild solution for the cooking process and found how to dry them out in a uniform time and method. He discovered a thinner, smaller pretzel was easier to bake, dry out, and pack properly. They also had a delicious flavor.

"He approached Ambrose Rauch to try the hard pretzels as a steady commercial item to sell in the big general stores. Mr. Rauch turned down the suggestion as he was getting along in years and didn't see any future in crispy, hard pretzels.

"Finally, Julius acquired a little shop to try out his ideas. Thus, in 1861, began the first "pretzels only" commercial pretzel bakery in the United States and probably the world.

"My Great Uncle Edwin worked with him and cried with him as he struggled to introduce hard pretzels. He would bake one day and get on his little delivery wagon the next day, trying to sell a few wooden boxes of hard pretzels to the stores. He nearly starved. He couldn't pay his wages or suppliers for weeks at a time and was more than once ready to throw in the sponge.

"Somehow he hung on. The first six or seven years were hard times without let up. Finally, the tide turned, and J. F. Sturgis Pretzels became a demand product.

"By 1880, he had two, and at times, three large two-horse, pretzel wagons delivering all over Lancaster, Lebanon, York, Chester, and parts of Berks County. He had a full-time man tending his horses and wagons. The work was done mostly at night, as the wagons were loaded and ready to go at 4:30 a.m.

"Julius Sturgis was handicapped. He was a cripple. He was kicked by a horse as a boy. His pelvis bones were damaged, and he limped all his life.

"He was also way ahead of his time on cleanliness. The bakery floors were scrubbed with soap and water at regular intervals. The wagons had to be washed because all roads were rather muddy.

"He taught his own bakers, mixers, and packers. He must have done quite well eventually as he owned a winter home in Florida where he spent three or four months each year. He also had a summer cottage in Mt. Gretna, Pennsylvania. He died in 1897 and is buried in the Moravian Church cemetery in Lititz, Pennsylvania.

"Since 1861, J. F. Sturgis, then a son or grandson has been baking pretzels without any intervals. I, my son, and my grandsons are the only direct descendants of Julius Sturgis, baking pretzels to this day [many] years since J. F. Sturgis started.

"Now I am going to throw a real sprag in the wheels of the historians and people who know all about it. Julius Sturgis did not start his bakery in 1861 at what is now the so-called original Julius Sturgis Bakery. He started in a little one-oven shop, one half block below the present site. Maybe the plaque should be moved…"

– Marriott ("Tom") Sturgis

The Sturgis Lineage

Alonzo Walton Sturges, an author, records the first Sturges family member on record in England 1530.

In 1630 the first Sturgises arrived in America from England. Edward Sturgis settled in Charlestown.

Joseph Sturgis, of English descent, was born March 16, 1738. He married Margaret Stohr, and they had seven sons and three daughters.

One of Joseph's sons was Samuel Justinius Sturgis, born in 1781.

One of Samuel's sons was Jacob Correll Sturgis, born in 1808.

Jacob's son was **Julius Ferdinand Sturgis**, born February 15, 1835, later the **founder of the first commercial pretzel bakery in America** in 1861. He operated this bakery till 1893. He died on October 4, 1897, at the age of 62.

The first bride of Julius, Miss Sarah Lint (1835-1876), was known as the "Beauty of the County." She gave him three sons and three daughters and then died in childbirth.

Their sons: Nathan, William, and Walter

Their daughters: Mary Ann, Clara, and Margie

Julius married a second wife, Sarah Oehme in 1878, and together they had two boys and two girls.

Their sons: Lewis and Homer

Their daughters: Martha and Sally

One of Julius's sons from his first marriage was William Augustus Sturgis, born 1867. William's first marriage produced one son: Willie. William married Mary Smith and had 5 boys and 11 girls:

Their sons: Charles, Chauncey, Correll, Arthur, and Marriott

Their daughters: Mary, Irene, Beulah, Ethel, Lillian, Mildred, Dorothy, Lucy, Thelma, Betty, and June

One of William's sons was Marriott Donald (Tom) Sturgis, born 1910, the original founder in 1946 of Tom Sturgis Pretzels. Marriott married Lottie and together they had only one son Thomas.

Thomas David Sturgis, born 1934, is the current CEO of Tom Sturgis Pretzels. Thomas and his wife Barbara have two sons and one daughter.

Their sons: Bruce and Chris
Their daughter: Jill

Bruce is currently the president of Tom Sturgis Pretzels, and Jill (author of this book) is the corporate secretary.

The children and grandchildren of Jill, Bruce, and Chris represent the sixth and seventh generation of Julius Sturgis' lineage, and some have already been participating in various capacities in the pretzel-making endeavor.

In front: Barbara / L-R Tom, Chris, Jill, Bruce

Summary of the Progression

In 1861, Julius Sturgis opened the first commercial pretzel bakery in the United States after developing the process of making crispy hard pretzels. The first bakery was in Lititz, Pennsylvania. This location now houses a museum and tour of the original bakery areas and is the sister company of Tom Sturgis Pretzels.

Julius Sturgis's sons assisted him in running the bakery as they became adults. One of his sons, William Sturgis, eventually founded his own pretzel bakery.

William Sturgis was the father of Marriott D. Sturgis. As Marriott became an adult he also worked in his father's bakery.

Marriott later joined his cousin Luke Miller and brother Correll to establish their own bakery in Reading, Pennsylvania. Most bakers were drafted into service during World War II, so the bakery closed its doors.

In 1946, Marriott Sturgis established "Tom Sturgis Pretzels" in a small building in the center of Reading.

Why was it called "Tom Sturgis Pretzels?"

As Marriott was developing his baking skills, he was told he baked like another more experienced baker, Tom Keller ("old Tom"). Many called Marriott "Tom," and the nickname stuck. For the rest of his life, he was "Tom" Sturgis.

Over the years, Marriott's son, Thomas D. Sturgis, joined the bakery, and eventually his children became involved too. Sixth and seventh generations are peeking from the wings and becoming involved now also.

As the business grew, the bakery moved several times in order to expand and add more modern equipment. Today, Tom Sturgis Pretzels, Inc. is located on the outskirts of Reading, Pennsylvania.

Over a century and a half of experience and seven generations later, we are still creating the tastiest pretzels in the land!

Pretzels and the Tom Sturgis Timeline

610 AD – Pretzels, "Pretiolas," first made in monastery in Southern France of Northern Italy

1500 AD – Pretzel bakers credited with saving Vienna, Austria, from siege by the Turks.

(**Note:** The following information was collected from Marriott D. Sturgis [grandson of Julius F. Sturgis] during two interviews on May 29, 1985 and May 31, 1985.)

1835 to 1897 – Julius was born February 15, 1835 and died October 4, 1897 at age 62. He was slightly crippled as a result of being kicked by a horse as a youth. Consequently, he held reserve status during the Civil War. Even so, he was called to active duty at the time of the Battle of Gettysburg in order to help defend or destroy the bridges over the Susquehanna River at Columbia, Pennsylvania.

1861 – Julius Ferdinand Sturgis (J. F. Sturgis) establishes the first commercial pretzel bakery at 219 East Main Street, Lititz, Pennsylvania. The bakery was an addition to his home.

1861 to 1893 – This original bakery was owned and operated by Julius F. Sturgis.

1893 – Nathan Sturgis (born 1865, died 1949), son of J. F. Sturgis, purchases the bakery with a partner Frank Buch.

1893 to 1910/1912 – Nathan Sturgis and Frank Buch operate the East Main Street, Lititz bakery.

1900 to 1950 – Homer Sturgis, half-brother of William A. Sturgis, operates a bakery with Dewey Haines called the Lititz Springs Pretzel Bakery, proprietors Sturgis and Haines. Jim Heebner founded this bakery.

1910/1912 – Nathan Sturgis becomes the sole owner of the East Main Street, Lititz bakery. William Augustus Sturgis (born 1867, died 1945), brother of Nathan, was the bakery plant foreman.

1910/1912 to 1940 – Nathan Sturgis's bakery is in continuous operation.

1918 to 1923 – William A. Sturgis establishes his own bakery in the rear of Cedar Street, Lititz, Pennsylvania.

1923 to 1931 – William A. Sturgis moves to Wyomissing, PA, and begins a bakery with his cousin Victor Sturgis, son of Nathan and Nathan's first wife. This bakery was on Hill Avenue, Wyomissing,

PA. Two brothers, Marriott D. (born 1910, died 1999) and Correll F. (born 1903, died 1980), sons of William A. Sturgis, worked at this bakery until 1929 or 1930.

1929/1930 to 1933 – Marriott And Correll Sturgis, brothers and sons of William A. Sturgis, build a bakery on Portland Avenue, West Wyomissing, PA. They used a portable oven to bake the pretzels. In 1933 this bakery was closed because of its poor location. The trucks became moored in muck almost daily because of the absence of paved streets.

1931 – Victor Sturgis had two bakeries in Reading, PA, on Green Street and Cotton Street.

1931 – William A. Sturgis retires.

1933 to 1937 – After vacating the West Wyomissing bakery, Marriott D. and Correll F. Sturgis move their baking operation to Hill Avenue, Wyomissing, PA, in the building vacated by Victor Sturgis and rent from Wyomissing Industries. In 1937 they receive notice that they must vacate the premises because Wyomissing Industries needs the area to create a parking lot.

1937 to 1942 – Marriott D. and Correll F. purchase a building on Penn Avenue, Wyomissing, on the north side of the 1300 block, near the old Wyomissing Fire Hall. They install a rotary-type oven. The bakery was closed because all employees were drafted into World War II service.

1946 – Marriott D. Sturgis buys a bakery on Grape Street, Reading, PA. **The "Tom Sturgis Pretzel Bakery" is born!**

1946 to 1948 or 1949 – Marriott D. operates the bakery on Grape Street. He uses a stationary brick oven.

1949 to 1952 – The Tom Sturgis Pretzels Bakery moves to Saul's Court, Reading. Pretzels are baked on a rotary soapstone hearth oven.

1952 to 1970 – The Tom Sturgis Pretzels Bakery moves to 700 Lancaster Avenue, Reading. Pretzels are still baked on a rotary soapstone hearth oven. Tom Sturgis Pretzels becomes incorporated on November 1, 1959.

1956 – Thomas D. Sturgis (born 1934), son of Marriott D. begins employment there.

1962 – Tom Sturgis Pretzels installs automatic twisting machines.

1970 to Present – Tom Sturgis Pretzels, Inc. builds a new bakery at 2267 Lancaster Pike, Reading. Pretzels are baked in tunnel soapstone-hearth ovens.

1981 – Bruce T. Sturgis (born 1959), son of Thomas D. Sturgis, grandson of Marriott D. Sturgis, begins employment there.

1985 – Chris A. Sturgis (born 1963), son of Thomas D. Sturgis, grandson of Marriott D. Sturgis, begins employment there. Chris leaves after several years to attend flight school. He currently flies Life Flight medical helicopters for local hospitals.

1987 – Tom Sturgis becomes president of the company.

1990 – Tom Sturgis Pretzels eliminates the pretzel twisting machines and installs extruders for forming pretzel shapes.

1998 – Tom Sturgis becomes CEO, and his son Bruce takes over as president.

2004 – Lindsay A. Adams, daughter of Jill M. Thomas and granddaughter of Thomas D. Sturgis, begins employment there.

2007 – On August 27 Tom Sturgis Pretzels regains control of Julius Sturgis' original bakery in Lititz and names it "Julius Sturgis Pretzel Bakery" where it is used as a museum and tourist attraction.

2011 – The company celebrates 150 years in business by hosting an extravagant Pretzel Party for the employees and community members. Over 2000 people attend.

2014 – Over the years the company has launched new products including soy-based pretzels and most recently in 2014, Tom Sturgis Pretzels launched "Julius Sturgis Horse and Buggy Pretzels."

FUN FOR THE FAMILY

Family Fun – Make Play Dough Pretzels

When you're looking for a fun, rainy day activity for the kiddos, consider whipping up a batch or two of colored play dough. Use the following easy play dough recipe.

Once the dough is made, test your skills making some pretzels. Roll out a thin strip of dough to about 15 inches. Follow the steps on page 31 of this book and twist your pretzel.

How fast can you twist? Remember, back in the early days of pretzel baking, twisters were skilled enough to twist up to forty pretzels a minute!

Play Dough Recipe

Ingredients:
2 cups flour
1 cup salt
4 teaspoons cream of tartar
2 cups cool water
2 tablespoons vegetable oil
Food coloring

Directions:
Combine the dry ingredients in a large bowl.
Whisk the wet ingredients together in a small bowl.
Add the wet mixture into the dry and stir until well combined.
Put the dough into a saucepan and cook it over low heat. Watch for a soft dough ball to form as you stir it. Remove from the heat when the dough is no longer sticky.
Put the dough ball onto a counter and knead it until it is smooth and soft. Flatten it and cool the dough for ten minutes. Knead again. Store in a plastic zip loc storage bag, squeezing out all the excess air.
Reminder: This dough is just for play. Do not eat!

Fun Pretzel Books for Families

Baptiste, Baron. *My Daddy is a Pretzel: Yoga for Parents and Kids.* Cambridge, MA: Barefoot Books, 2012.

Carle, Eric. *Walter the Baker.* New York, NY: Aladdin Paperbacks, Simon & Schuster Children's Publishing Division, 1995.

Hunt, Angela Elwell. *Pretzels by the Dozen: Truth and Inspiration with a Heart-Shaped Twist.* Grand Rapids, MI: Zondervan, Zonderkidz Division, 2002.

McKain, Susan and Swann, Sandy. *Tugger, the Pretzel Pup.* Bloomington, IN: AuthorHouse, 2010.

Pinkwater, Daniel and Jill. *The Werewolf Club #1: The Magic Pretzel.* New York, NY: Aladdin Paperbacks, Simon & Schuster Children's Publishing Division, 2000.

Rey, Margret. *Pretzel.* Boston, MA: Houghton Mifflin Harcourt, 1997.

Sachs, Marilyn. *Amy Moves In.* Bloomington, IN: iUniverse, 2001. (Note: Although this book isn't completely about pretzels, there is one chapter that is.)

Smucker, Anna Egan. *Brother Giovanni's Little Reward: How the Pretzel Was Born.* Grand Rapids, MI: Eerdmans Books for Young Readers, 2015.

CONTACT
INFORMATION

Tom Sturgis Pretzels (factory and retail store)
2267 Lancaster Pike
Reading, PA 19607-2498
800-777-3314 or 610-775-0335
www.tomsturgispretzels.com
Facebook: Tom Sturgis Pretzels

Located just off Route 222 in Shillington, our retail store is open to the public Monday through Saturday, 8:30 a.m. to 5:30 p.m. Buses are welcome.

Enjoy samples of all our pretzels while you browse. Guests can purchase our full product line of pretzels as well as a variety of gift items. Mail order gifts are also available.

Julius Sturgis Pretzel House and Museum
219 East Main Street
Lititz, PA 17543
717-626-4354
http://juliussturgis.com/visitus.html
Facebook: Julius Sturgis Pretzel Bakery

Step back in time with a visit to the historic bakery in Lititz and get a glimpse of what it was like for Julius Sturgis to bake pretzels in the "old days." Your visit will be informative and fun with interactive demonstrations, photographs, and historical equipment. Take a tour of the old bakery area and learn to twist a pretzel.

Author Jill Marie Thomas

Website, Blog, Bookstore: www.jillmariethomas.com
Facebook: Jill Thomas and Jill Marie Thomas
Instagram: @jillgoes

To inquire about booking Jill Marie Thomas for a speaking
engagement, please email the author at: jillgoes@gmail.com

Made in the
USA
Middletown, DE